Original title:
Tropical Moonlight

Copyright © 2025 Creative Arts Management OÜ
All rights reserved.

Author: Adeline Fairfax
ISBN HARDBACK: 978-1-80581-521-1
ISBN PAPERBACK: 978-1-80581-048-3
ISBN EBOOK: 978-1-80581-521-1

An Island's Heartbeat in Darkness

In the night a coconut fell,
It startled a crab, oh what a yell!
The waves chuckled, a soft tease,
As lizards danced with wobbly knees.

A parrot squawked, a comical tune,
While moody fish swam to the moon.
Palms whispered jokes in the breeze,
Making even the shadows sneeze.

The Cauldron of Dreams Beneath Stars

A turtle rapped on a seashell phone,
While a gull snored away on a lone stone.
Jellyfish twinkled, oh what a show,
As crabs played tag, then tripped on their toe.

Starlit whispers filled the night air,
While otters giggled without a care.
The cocktails served in clamshells bright,
Left even the clouds rolling in delight.

Coffee-Scented Breezes at Midnight

Nighttime brews in a coconut cup,
Sipping, we watch the fireflies hop.
A sloth grumbles while napping nearby,
Dreaming of races, oh my, oh my!

Breeze tickles noses, scents so divine,
Each gulp of brew feels like sunshine.
A monkey would dance, but first, a snack,
His shimmy's so funny, we almost crack.

The Brief, Fleeting Hour of Shadows

A bat zoomed by—what a fast flier!
While geckos jived, their moves couldn't tire.
Shadows played hopscotch under the trees,
As a toucan giggled and flapped with ease.

Amid the laughter, a bowl rolled away,
And crabs called bingo! at the end of the bay.
The hour flowed by with jokes on the run,
Until dawn tiptoed, saying, "Wasn't that fun?"

The Rhythm of the Evening Tide

Under the stars, the crabs all dance,
They twirl and spin, if given a chance.
With shells that shine, they take their stand,
Making a party on the wet sand.

Laughing gulls join in with a shout,
The fishermen hope they won't find out.
While waves clap hands in a frothy cheer,
The moon just smiles, with a wink, my dear.

Glimmers on the Horizon

A fish with sunglasses swims by me,
Bobbing along, so carefree and free.
It gives a wink, and oh, what a sight,
As jellyfish glide in their own sleight!

Dolphins in bow ties frolic with glee,
As waves hum a tune just for thee.
They flip and they flop with such flair,
The ocean's a show, beyond compare!

Petals Whispered by the Wind

In the breeze, the flowers conspire,
Setting petals alight with desire.
They giggle and sway, too shy to show,
That the bees are their fans at the big show!

With pollen jokes and sweet serenades,
They tease the butterflies in shady glades.
The sun nods along with a golden grin,
As petals prance, let the fun begin!

Flickering Lanterns in the Dark

Lanterns swing like ghosts in the night,
Each bulb a face, giggling with fright.
They gather in clusters, sharing the light,
Trading dad jokes beneath the moon's sight!

A wild dance begins on the sandy floor,
As glowworms swarm and beg for more.
The night is alive, with laughter and cheer,
As flickering friends draw everyone near!

A Canvas of Night Painted in Memories

Under the beams of a silvery sheen,
Laughter erupts where the palm trees lean.
A crab with no rhythm danced on the shore,
While a coconut fell with a soft little roar.

The breeze brings whispers of stories untold,
Of fisherman dreams and their catches so bold.
We giggle at shadows that silently sway,
While the stars above wink and giggle in play.

A hammock sways low like a giant's big grin,
As we aim for the moon, but we fall with a spin.
The night comes alive with a splash and a cheer,
Dancing on sand, pulling memories near.

So let's raise a toast to the laughs in the dark,
To the moments we share, every quirk, every spark.
With friends by our side and a heart full of cheer,
We paint the night bright with our joy and our beer.

Beneath Stars, in the Island's Embrace

Beneath the bright twinkle of diamonds so high,
A peculiar parrot attempts to fly by.
With a squawk and a wobble, it lands by my side,
Dropping its treasure, that smelly old tide!

The waves giggle softly, tickling the sand,
While a dog on the beach draws up lines in the sand.
Clapping our hands at the antics so bold,
We forget about night, only laughter we hold.

A sombrero flies off, sails into the air,
Chasing the moonlight without any care.
As we dance with the shadows, our feet fly and twirl,
We tumble like seashells in a playful whirl.

To the rhythm of waves and the soft ocean's sigh,
In the glow of the night, we let worries pass by.
In the island's embrace, we frolic and roam,
Creating our joy, in this paradise home.

The Sound of Silent Wishes

Twinkling stars dance in skies,
Where laughter and whispers fly.
A coconut falls with a thud,
I laugh as I dodge the dud.

Seashells wear hats made of foam,
While fish joke about their home.
A crab walks sideways with flair,
Trying to dance like it's rare.

Bananas play hide and seek,
As monkeys chatter and squeak.
The light has a goofy glow,
Making shadows steal the show.

In this land of bright delight,
Even the moon smiles at night.
Silent wishes wrapped in glee,
Float along like jellyfish free.

Melodies at Seaside Altar

Waves crashing with a cheeky grin,
While sea turtles laugh and spin.
Pelicans flap and take flight,
Singing tunes for pure delight.

Bamboo flutes made from tall grass,
Humming softly as crabs pass.
Jellyfish waltz in the brine,
While mermaids sip sweet divine.

Pineapple hats on the sand,
Cool drinks served up by a band.
Coconuts hold secret songs,
As seaweed sways, where it belongs.

Under lights of dazzling stars,
Humor shines like little cars.
At the altar of the waves,
Joy is found in the playful caves.

Refractions of Wonder Underneath

Under water, colors play,
Bubbles laugh as they sway.
A fish grins with a big, wide smile,
While octopuses dance in style.

A treasure chest opens to show,
A rubber duck ready to go.
The sea cucumbers bring the charms,
With sea urchins waving their arms.

Playful dolphins jump with grace,
Wearing seaweed like a lace.
Crabs tell jokes about their day,
As sunsets turn the skies to clay.

In the deep where secrets freeze,
Even jellyfish float with ease.
Reflections jiggle on the reef,
Making laughter the main motif.

The Edge of Night's Mystery

On the shore where shadows play,
Seagulls snicker and sway.
Stars elope with a wink,
Sipping moonlight from the brink.

Laughter echoes through the palms,
Fireflies glow, bringing calms.
A raccoon winks with a grin,
As night begins to spin.

Frogs croak jokes from the bog,
While turtles dance on a log.
The night whispers silly rhymes,
Turning waves into giggling chimes.

At the edge where dreams unite,
Even the crickets sing with might.
Mysterious, yet so clear,
Fun and laughter float near.

The Call of Distant Drums

In the jungle where parrots shout,
A beat of drums makes them jump about.
Monkeys laugh and shake their heads,
Chasing shadows where mischief spreads.

The rhythm tickles their furry feet,
As they dance to the tune of a funny beat.
Lizards snicker as they glide,
While gophers giggle, unable to hide.

Crickets chirp in silly sync,
Adding a tune to make you think.
The night is young, the laughter loud,
Jungle creatures form a quirky crowd.

So come and join the wild parade,
With joyful antics, no debts unpaid.
Here in the dark, there's nothing serious,
Just fun and drums that sound delirious.

Illumination in the Canopy

Under the leaves that catch a ray,
The critters plan a silly play.
Fireflies flicker like neon stars,
As iguanas argue over who drives cars.

The sloths slow dance in awkward style,
While toucans squawk as they reconcile.
Chasing their tails, the butterflies swirl,
Making the scene a comical whirl.

A raccoon's eyes twinkle in jest,
While the honking geese are on a quest.
To find the snacks that squirrels hid,
Cheeky and bright, they forget what they did.

So here among the beams so bright,
Let laughter echo into the night.
The canopy's secrets, all wrapped in fun,
With whims and whimsy, the night's just begun.

The Last Light of Day's Embrace

As daylight fades, the antics rise,
With giggles hidden in each surprise.
Chameleons change in a flash of green,
Making the night look like a screen.

The sun slips down with a cheeky grin,
While the frogs croak out a silly din.
A parrot sings, but it's out of tune,
Dancing alone under the soft moon.

A quick-footed deer jumps through the scene,
Trying so hard to stay unseen.
But bumblebees buzz with delighted cheer,
As a patchy dog dives into the sphere.

So soak in the silliness, the playful tease,
The night's in a whirl; let laughter breeze.
In this fading light of the day's own dance,
Each creature dons a comical chance.

Moonbeams Through Canopy Leaves

When the beams break through the thick of trees,
Lemurs frolic while with such ease.
Street lights jump, the stars make fun,
As night's wild antics have just begun.

Fuzzy raccoons gather 'round,
Trying to be the silliest in town.
With acorn hats and leafy clothes,
They're kings and queens of the evening's shows.

A crab crawls by with a toothy wink,
He's got his moves and they're on the brink.
With laughter echoing in the night,
They dance and prance with pure delight.

So come and watch this merry crew,
Leave your worries behind, bid adieu.
With joy in the air and laughter leaves,
The fun is wrapped in moonlit eaves.

Gentle Touch of the Evening Tide

When the waves tickle your toes,
Seashells giggle in the dark,
Fishes dance in silly rows,
And crabs clap to the sparking lark.

Coconut palms sway with glee,
As the parrot tells a joke,
Dolphins leap in harmony,
While the starfish learns to croak.

The glow of sandlights flickers bright,
A crab wears shades — quite the sight!
Laughter echoes, soft and light,
As moonbeams shine on every bite.

So grab your friend, let's make a mess,
We'll splash around, no need to stress.
Dance beneath that sparkly dress,
Of night-time fun, no need to guess!

Dreaming on a Feathered Breeze

Feathers float on gentle air,
While monkeys swing with cheeky grins.
Parrots squawk without a care,
Chasing dreams as daylight thins.

Coconuts fall like soft rain,
Landing on a dancing frog.
Laughter bursts like summer grain,
Echoing through the happy fog.

The owl in glasses reads a book,
While crickets play a jazzy tune.
Underneath the starry nook,
Turtles join, a silly croon.

Floating dreams on waves of fun,
Imagination takes its flight.
Here, beneath the moon we've spun,
Every moment glimmers bright!

Whispers of the Night Breeze

In the dark, the fireflies tease,
While the moon wears a silver grin.
Bamboo sways in softest breeze,
Tickling toes of the turtle kin.

Lizards gossip with a sway,
Each tale's funnier than the last.
They share tales of their wild play,
While sipping nectar from the past.

The waves sing melodies of lore,
As the beach ball rolls with mirth,
Sandy sculptures stand in score,
Claiming their giggles as their worth.

With each whisper of the night,
The breeze carries giggles anew.
Join the humor, feel the light,
Underneath this sky so blue!

Celestial Reflections on Still Waters

Stars dance on a shimmering lake,
While frogs put on their best show.
Lily pads swish, then break,
As fish swim by in fancy flow.

Gazing at the mirrored sky,
A turtle dons a tiny hat.
Crickets bow as fireflies fly,
Making wishes, where's my cat?

The breeze tells jokes with a wink,
As the moon grins down below.
Clouds giggle, never think,
About drama in the glow.

So splash and laugh, come take a ride,
On these waters of mirth and cheer.
In this world where dreams collide,
And joy is found in every sphere!

Symphony of the Midnight Lagoon

In the stillness, frogs croak cheer,
Donkeys dance without a care.
Crabs do the cha-cha in the sand,
While fish tease with a playful hand.

Coconuts drop with a thud, oh dear,
Swaying palms seem to smirk and leer.
A parrot sings out of tune,
Swirling with the dancing moon.

Mischief stirs in the night so bright,
As critters giggle, taking flight.
Laughter bubbles, it shimmies and sways,
In this aquatic, wacky ballet.

Giggling waves in the lagoon's embrace,
Light-hearted creatures join the race.
Jellyfish float with silly glee,
In this nighttime jubilee.

Rays of Moonlight on Paradise Sands

On the shore where sunbathers flop,
A seagull steals a snack, so nonchalant.
Sandy toes and flip-flops dance,
While crabs mimic a limping prance.

Flip-flops fly in a comic arc,
As a beach ball lands with a spark.
Picnics turn into food fights grand,
Who knew that sand was a spicy blend?

The lifeguard snoozes, dreams of fame,
While kids plot victories in their game.
Sunburned noses twinkling bright,
Turn sagas of mischief by night.

As stars peek in, the pranks unfold,
With shadows laughing, the bold and the old.
With glee we gather, our joy takes flight,
Under the watch of the cheerful night.

Beneath the Canopy of Stars

Beneath the stars, we trip and roll,
An octopus paints on a giant shoal.
Mangroves giggle in the gentle breeze,
While turtles wager who'll eat the cheese.

Laughter erupts, it echoes so wide,
As geckos join in the moonlit slide.
The air is sweet with tales to tell,
As critters spin their funny spell.

Coconuts launch with comedy flair,
As coconut crabs dance here and there.
Fireflies twinkle like disco lights,
As we relish this wacky night.

Under the canopy, we laugh till dawn,
In a world where silliness is never gone.
Where every shadow has a dance to make,
Beneath the stars, for laughter's sake.

The Glistening Whisper of Dusk

As dusk unfolds, the mischief brews,
With crickets chirping their lively blues.
A raccoon dons a hat so grand,
While innuendo dances, quite out of hand.

Vines creeping close, they seem to tease,
With snakes who curl, never to please.
The moon whispers secrets, cleverly sly,
While frogs gather 'round to give it a try.

In this twilight, a chorus of gags,
With pufferfish puffing like comical flags.
The water twinkles, a wink on the bay,
As creatures unwinding, chase day away.

Laughter and splashes fill the night air,
As we wade through bosoms of playful despair.
With every ripple, we revel and cheer,
For the night's embrace is cozy and dear.

Moonlit Tidepool Reverie

Crabs dance a jig on the slick rocks,
As starfish giggle in their beachy socks.
A clam sings loudly, proud of its shell,
While the seaweed sways, oh, what a swell!

The moon winks down with a silvery tease,
Fishes are laughing, just doing as they please.
Oysters are gossiping, pearls in their grip,
While jellyfish float by, giving it a flip.

A seagull swoops low, it joins in the fun,
Telling fish tales beneath the bright sun.
With every splash and every spree,
This tidepool is wild as wild can be!

Bubbles arise like giggles in the night,
Stars in the sky shine down with delight.
As the waves crash in, we know this is true:
Tidepool parties are the best kind of zoo!

Shadows of Paradise

Beneath the palms where the coconuts fall,
A monkey's doing its best to enthrall.
With a hat of leaves perched on its head,
It juggles mangoes, oh, what a spread!

Geckos are grinning on sun-warmed stone,
While turtles are gossiping, not quite alone.
Parrots caw loudly, sharing a joke,
As laughter erupts from a nearby oak.

In this paradise where shadows do play,
The rhythm of life finds its humorous way.
Even the breeze sings a silly refrain,
Chatting with flowers, not one is in strain.

Mirth in the air like the scent of sweet blooms,
Laughter erupts from the beach as it looms.
As night starts to fall and the stars make a fuss,
This silly spectacle is contagious to us!

A Lullaby for the Stars

Crickets are chirping their nightly refrain,
While fireflies flicker like dancers in vain.
The ocean hums softly, a tune from below,
As dreams take a flight in the moon's gentle glow.

A frog in its fancy dives in with a splash,
Singing of wishes, it makes quite the dash.
With each little croak, the stars start to sway,
Bouncing along through the milky way.

The breeze tells a story, a giggly delight,
As shadows are stretching, preparing for night.
With a wink and a nod, the moon softly beams,
In this lullaby land, we dance in our dreams.

So close your eyes, dear, let silliness reign,
For the stars are your buddies, never mundane.
In this nighttime revelry, laughter will guide,
As we drift through the cosmos on a shimmering tide.

Driftwood Dreams Under a Silver Sky

Old driftwood lies like a wise old sage,
Telling jokes to the waves, turning a page.
With barnacles laughing, the joke's never old,
As the beach whispers secrets in shades of gold.

A crab with a top hat struts with great pride,
While lizards play poker, their backs to the tide.
Pelicans giggle, they float on the sea,
Sharing fish tales - oh, what company!

The pebbles all chuckle in bright colored hues,
As the night winds down with a sigh and a snooze.
Under this canvas of twinkling delight,
Driftwood keeps dreaming, a heart full of light.

So come, take a seat, join this hilarious show,
Where the sand tickles toes and the waves steal the glow.
Tonight is a riot, full of love and surprise,
Under the laughter that falls from the skies!

Reflections in the Warm Tides

The ocean's gleam, a shiny smile,
Crabs dance about, and all the while,
A jellyfish in a disco groove,
Flips and flops, oh, what a move!

Seashells giggle on the shore,
They plot and plan, they want some more,
A conch shell sings a silly song,
To all the fish who hum along.

Waves tickle toes in playful jest,
While seagulls squawk, they know their best,
With seaweed wigs that sway and sway,
They join the fun, they steal the day.

The moonlight shines like buttercream,
Dreams drift by on a wobbly beam,
With laughter echoing all around,
In this fun land, joy is abound!

Secrets of the Underworld Revealed

The octopus wears a tiny hat,
He greets a whale, who's quite the brat,
With bubbles popping like balloons,
They dance beneath the sun and moons.

Eels that whisper in the deep,
Tell secrets that will make you weep,
A grouchy crab with a scowlful face,
Joins in a conga, finds his place.

The sea floor's buzzing with delight,
A party brewing, oh, what a sight,
Anemones sway with style so bold,
While sea cucumbers break the mold.

Fish tell tales with flamboyant flair,
Gossip spreads all through the air,
In this underwater carnival spree,
Laughs resound in the salty sea!

Romance Amidst the Boughs

In trees that twist with gentle heart,
Squirrels flirt with impish art,
A couple of birds compose a tune,
With love notes sent beneath the moon.

A chameleon winks with sly intent,
He paints his scales for the love he's sent,
While frogs croak sweet in a lover's croon,
A serenade for the stars up soon.

Leaves rustle in a giggling breeze,
A cuddle of vines in playful tease,
With fireflies twinkling, what a sight,
Their love is bright, a flirtatious light.

The night unfolds with laughter sweet,
Nature's ball, where all hearts meet,
In twilight's glow, antics take flight,
Romance reigns through the merry night!

A Tapestry of Stars Above

Stars twinkle like mischief in the sky,
They play peek-a-boo, oh my, oh my,
An astronaut cat floats on high,
Chasing a comet that whizzes by.

Constellations sing a silly song,
While meteors dash, they hurry along,
A bear with sunglasses makes a scene,
On the Milky Way's far-off screen.

Galactic giggles echo bright,
As aliens dance in pure delight,
With cosmic parties, they spin and sway,
Creating adventures that come what may.

Beneath this quilt of wonder grand,
Laughter spills from starry hand,
In the universe's playful dome,
Every twinkle feels like home!

In the Embrace of Canopy Silence

In the jungle, monkeys dance with glee,
Cheeky chatter rises high in the trees.
A parrot squawks in sneaky surprise,
While everyone else pretends to be wise.

Crickets play tunes on their tiny strings,
As fireflies flicker and do little flings.
The moon's a comedian, shining so bright,
It giggles with shadows, delighting the night.

Lizards are lounging, wearing sunglasses,
Sipping on nectar from flowered glasses.
A sloth joins in with unhurried charm,
Wishing he could dance but means no harm.

Beneath leafy covers, laughter takes flight,
In the embrace of silence, everything's light.

Echoes of Tomorrow in the Stars

Stars in the sky wink mischievously down,
But one star fell early and rolled through town.
It tripped on a cloud, much to its surprise,
And landed in laughter under wide-open skies.

Planets are gossiping, sharing their dreams,
While comets are racing with sparkly beams.
An asteroid grumbles, 'What's all this fuss?'
While a meteor zooms yelling, 'Catch up with us!'

The moon is the DJ, spinning tunes to the night,
With craters for speakers making it all tight.
Galaxies twirl, a cosmic ballet,
Even time itself decides to play.

In the vastness, humor's a wild guest,
Echoes of tomorrow bring out the best.

When Time Slows Under Moonlit Haze

The night air's thick, as if time forgot,
A turtle named Timmy forgot his spot.
He stumbled on shadows, what a sight to see,
Claiming he's fast, but we'll wait and see!

Bats are out shopping for stylish capes,
While owls in coats discuss new escape tapes.
And frogs throw parties with croaking delight,
Mixing drinks under soft, shimmering light.

The moon plays tricks with its dreamy glow,
Making tree trunks appear like a dance show.
Grasshoppers hop to marry the breeze,
While fireflies compete in sparkly degrees.

In this laid-back waltz where laughter's the prize,
Time slows down, wearing a silly disguise.

The Art of Night in Vibrant Hues

The night paints colors with a laugh and a twist,
Where shadows and giggles in fun coexist.
A painter in pajamas mixes the shades,
Splashing the sky with playful cascades.

Each star's a brushstroke, so bold, so bright,
While clouds are the canvases dancing with light.
A raccoon critiques, with a monocle neat,
Saying, 'This artwork could use a bit more beat!'

Chameleons dance in their polka-dot shoes,
Tickling the colors that nature imbues.
A parade of critters, with hats made of leaves,
Celebrate night while the world softly breathes.

In vibrant hues, the night's merry play,
Turning moments into a glorious array.

Night Fragrance in the Warmth

The air is thick with scents so sweet,
Like candy shops, all in one treat.
Bugs have gathered, what a sight!
Dancing wildly, oh what a fright!

Laughter echoes through the trees,
As lizards hop with utmost ease.
A crab does moonwalk, quite the show,
Silly antics, high and low!

The stars poked fun at all the fuss,
As coconut jokes made us discuss.
Who knew the night would be so bright?
With giggles carried into the night!

In every shadow, critters prance,
While we indulge in moonlit dance.
And as we sip on fruity drinks,
We giggle more than anyone thinks!

Chasing Shadows Under the Palm Leaves

Palm leaves sway as we take flight,
In a comedy, absurd delight.
My friend tripped on a flip-flop hose,
And now the party's in full prose!

We dance and leap among the gloom,
As shadows twist and take up room.
A coconut falls, we duck and weave,
It's like a game we can't believe!

The stars above begin to wink,
At all our silly speeches, pink.
We giggle at the cat's swift scoff,
Then wonder if the palm will cough!

With laughter echoing through the night,
We chase our shadows, what a sight!
The moon beams down on our parade,
This joyful mess, we'll never trade!

Serenade of the Mysterious Ocean

The ocean hums a goofy tune,
As crabs join in with a silly swoon.
A dolphin splashes joy and cheer,
While starfish giggle far and near.

With every wave's a chuckle loud,
A fish can't swim—oh, what a crowd!
Seagulls squawk in cartoonish tones,
As laughing shells make silly moans!

We find a treasure, oh so bright,
A shiny bauble, what a sight!
But wait! It's just a lost old shoe,
The ocean plays tricks, it's nothing new!

In the moonlight's glimmer, we dive deep,
As we disturb a giant heap.
With jokes and giggles in the sea,
We serenade our folly free!

Voyage of the Moon-Kissed Waves

Set sail on a boat made of dreams,
With laughter floating on starry beams.
A parrot squawks the wrong command,
As we drift off to a wonderland!

The waves giggle, bump and sway,
While creatures pop in for a play.
"Keep it steady!" I shout with glee,
As mermaids laugh at our clumsy spree!

Crabs play fiddles made of seaweed,
While squids perform at lightning speed.
Oh what a spectacle, pure delight,
The ocean's stage is shining bright!

Through moonlit paths, we lose our way,
But it's a game that we must play.
With every splash, we shout hooray,
This voyage brings us endless play!

The Symphony of Crickets' Song

Under the cloak of night, they play,
Crickets chirping in a grand array.
Their tunes so loud, they laugh and cheer,
While I dance around, sipping a beer.

Each note a whisper of summer's bliss,
They serenade me with a chirpy kiss.
With every hop, they start a new tune,
Who knew they'd be the stars of the June?

I tap my feet to their wobbly beat,
My dog joins in, with his own little feat.
He howls away, thinks he's a star,
While crickets judge him from near and far.

In this orchestra of winks and gleams,
Nature strums the heart deep in dreams.
So here I sit, in this wild bazaar,
With crickets composing under the star.

Midnight Wanderlust in the Tropics

I sneak outside while the world's fast asleep,
Catching fireflies in jars, a light in a leap.
They jive and swerve, having their own ball,
While I trip over roots, trying not to fall.

A coconut lies, asking for a ride,
I name him Pierre, my new fruity guide.
Together we scamper, through leaves and vines,
Ignoring the biting of little mean signs.

The moon winks at us, a cheeky old chap,
And I do a tango, complete with a clap.
Pierre rolls and tumbles, giggles abound,
In this midnight frolic, joy knows no bound.

With laughter we bounce, all the way till dawn,
Wandering where the wild shadows yawn.
Two pals on a mission, silly and bright,
Living it up in the magic of night.

A Polished Sea under Starlit Skies

The ocean winks under a sky full of sparks,
Splashes of laughter with the waves' playful arcs.
I look for mermaids, but they hide away,
Too busy Instagramming, what can I say?

The sea shimmers, a giant disco ball,
And I twirl like a fish, having a ball.
Kicking up sand with a joyous shout,
Who knew that beach life could be so sprout?

Seashells giggle as they cover my toes,
While seagulls squawk gossiping all that they know.
They squabble like friends in a silly debate,
As I munch on popcorn, the tide's funny fate.

The night draws close, I wave goodbye,
To my underwater friends with a sigh.
In this polished sea where laughter ignites,
Even the stars blink with joyful delights.

Gentle Ripples of Memory

Ripples of giggles cascade down the stream,
Memories dance, like a funny daydream.
Once I tripped over a big rock in the sun,
Fell in, made a splash, and oh, what fun!

The ducks quacked loudly, sure had their say,
As I soaked my shoes in a clumsy display.
They flapped their wings, giving me the look,
And I laughed so hard, I lost my good book.

The soft breeze carried my chuckles so light,
Mixing my giggles with the dark of the night.
A floating leaf waved like it knew my plight,
Telling me whisper tales of pure delight.

Each gentle ripple carries a jest,
In the heart of the night, I'm truly blessed.
With laughter and echoes forever set free,
These silly memories dance in my sea.

The Night's Caress on Sun-Kissed Skin

The breeze whispers sweet jokes,
As the stars giggle loud,
Silly crabs dance on the sand,
While the moon plays dress-up shroud.

Seagulls sharing their finest tales,
With fish that swim in disguise,
A pineapple on my head, I sway,
Under twinkling, watchful eyes.

Laughter bubbles with each wave,
As coconuts join in a cheer,
Who knew the ocean had a punchline?
The moon's winks spark the atmosphere!

Grinning stars sprinkle the sky,
Wrapping me in laughter's glow,
With every splash, the world giggles,
In the night where silliness flows.

Shadow Play Beneath Blossoms

In the jungle, shadows prance,
Bouncing like kids with no care,
A monkey swings, takes a glance,
While flowers gossip, unaware.

Lemurs dressed in fancy hats,
Disco under paper trees,
With rustling leaves providing beats,
And petals dancing in the breeze.

A parrot squawks a riddle loud,
While blossoms sway and tease,
Who knew that nature's a clown?
In this garden of buzzing bees!

I laugh until the sun rises,
With shadows still doing the dance,
Who knew the night could be this fun?
In the dark, we take a chance!

The Soft Glow of Bioluminescent Shores

Tiny lights in the water giggle,
As I paddle through the glow,
Starry sprites in a moonlit jiggle,
Whispering secrets from below.

Sea turtles with glowing necklaces,
Doing the cha-cha along the tide,
A jellyfish with a twinkle crest,
Teasing each wave as they glide.

With each splash, a spark of laughter,
Making ripples with every cheer,
Dancing waves, the ocean's crafter,
Bringing joy with every clear.

So let's toast to this liquid fun,
Under skies of glittering dreams,
Where even the night has a sense of humor,
In this place where light beams.

Dancing Light and Gentle Waves

The ocean hums a silly song,
As I bounce along the shore,
With moonbeams shining all night long,
Keeping us laughing forevermore.

Waves tickle my toes in glee,
A clam joins in for a laugh,
Who knew sea life could be so free?
As it forms a silly photograph!

The starfish poses with a wink,
While a sea urchin tells a tale,
Each tide burst, a frothy drink,
Filling the air with a spree that will not pale.

So let's twirl till sunrise appears,
With giggles bouncing from the sea,
For in this light of dancing cheers,
We find joy where we ought to be!

Whispers of the Island Night

Coconuts laugh upon the trees,
As crabs play tag with the evening breeze.
A parrot squawks, thinking it's sly,
While the moon winks, floating up high.

The sand tickles toes, oh what a delight,
As palm fronds sway, keeping spirits light.
A lizard struts, with a dapper flair,
While the stars giggle, hanging up there.

The sea bubbles up with a frothy grin,
As fish wear shades in a cheeky spin.
A turtle giggles, what a sight to see,
Bobbing along, just as happy as can be.

Boys chase the crabs, with clumsy glee,
While the night sings a song, oh so free.
The island's charm, a humorous spree,
In this bright tapestry, nothing else could be.

Luminous Waves Beneath the Stars

Under a sky of sparkling jewels,
The ocean dances, breaking the rules.
Waves giggle as they tickle the shore,
Whispering secrets, urging for more.

A fish dons a hat made of seaweed,
While a clam insists it's got the best speed.
Shells chuckle softly, feel the embrace,
As the moon throws a party, lighting the space.

Seashells play music, a shell-abration,
With crabs dancing in joyful elation.
Starfish spin tales, vivid and wide,
As the water swirls, like a carnival tide.

The breeze hums along, it's a feel-good jam,
A dolphin leaps high, oh, what a slam!
Laughter echoes through the night so bright,
As waves whisper jokes, a rib-tickling sight.

Siren's Call in Silver Hues

A mermaid giggles, tousled hair aglow,
Singing sweet tunes that ebb to and fro.
Fish gather round, all wearing big grins,
As seaweed wraps gifts, where the fun begins.

An octopus juggles pearls with great flair,
While seahorses dance, a comical pair.
The sea foam bubbles, tickling the toes,
As laughter and mischief gracefully flows.

Bright bubbles pop, what a funny sound,
A crab with a crown, prancing around.
The tides pull back, then rush in with a flash,
While stars throw confetti in a sparkling splash.

Under the glow of the silver sheen,
Everything's lively, quite the scene!
Even the twilight joins in the fun,
As night takes charge, and antics are spun.

Dance of the Coconut Palms

Coconut palms sway with a jolly twist,
Shaking their tops like they can't resist.
The wind tells jokes as it whistles by,
Making the branches tap and sigh.

A monkey swings through, wearing a grin,
Challenging the wind to a dizzying spin.
The bananas chuckle, hanging so low,
While coconuts murmur, 'Let's go with the flow!'

Palm leaves whisper, a rustling cheer,
As the moon's bright smile draws us near.
Crickets play tunes with a rhythmic beat,
While the island dances, oh what a treat!

Hula hoops made of vines whiz around,
As laughter erupts, a jubilant sound.
Clapping hands and tapping feet,
In the dance of the palms, the night feels complete.

Essence of Paradise in Twilight

In the evening glow, bananas dance,
Coconuts begin their wobbly prance.
Chickens in sunglasses strut with flair,
While palm trees chuckle in the salty air.

With every wave, the giggles grow,
As tourists trip on sand, oh no!
Laughter echoes, a joyful sound,
As sea turtles join, twirling around.

The crabs, they clap, the fish, they flip,
A limbo contest on a banana boat trip.
Underneath the stars wearing bright hats,
It's a party with skunks and flamingo spats.

As the moon grins wide like a fussy child,
Even the winds seem a bit more wild.
Come join the fun, don't miss your chance,
In this paradise, everyone can dance!

Lost in the Maze of Fronds

In the jungle dense with giggles and glee,
I tripped on a vine, oh, woe was me!
Parrots snickered in shades of green,
As monkeys juggled coconuts unseen.

Swatting at mosquitoes that wore tiny shoes,
I searched for a path, but oh my, what ruse!
A toucan chuckled, giving me a wink,
'Lost in the maze, what do you think?'

With every twist, I met a new friend,
A lazy iguana who just wouldn't blend.
'Stay with me, buddy, it's a wild ride,
In this feathery chaos, let's slip and slide!'

Finally escaped, I laughed with relief,
Finding my way was quite a belief.
The breeze blew soft; my heart's now a song,
In the world of leaves, I truly belong!

Nightfall's Palette of Colors

As the sun dipped low, the sky's a tease,
Painting the heavens like a piece of cheese.
Violets and oranges in a lively swirl,
As geckos in sunglasses do a slow twirl.

The waves hum tunes of wild delight,
While crickets conduct the orchestra of night.
A mango-shaped moon takes its place on high,
Winking at lovers who giggle and sigh.

With each splash, the colors blend bright,
A canvas of laughter under starry light.
A flamingo's legs, they break into song,
And even the crabs wave along, so strong.

So let your heart flutter, feel the fun grow,
As the night fills with colors that dance to and fro.
In this dreamscape, joy finds a way,
To paint us all happy, come what may!

The Portrait of a Distant Island

From afar I see a land of cheer,
Where pineapples wear hats and share a beer.
In the sky, cloud sheep are fluffing around,
While sea turtles sail with a giggly sound.

The sand, it sparkles like glitter in glee,
As the ocean waves shout, 'Come swim with me!'
The palm trees wave, their fronds all aflutter,
As a crab in a bow tie starts to strut.

With each playful ripple, the laughter spreads,
Even the dolphins flaunt colorful threads.
From colorful sunsets to coconuts' sway,
Even the fishes join the frolicking fray.

Oh, this portrait of fun, a landscape of play,
Where shadows and light dance night into day.
Let's sip on the joy that the island imparts,
For in this bright paradise, we share silly hearts!

Echoes of the Nightingale's Call

A bird with a flair sings out with a cheer,
Chasing away worries, and tickling the ear.
With bananas for feet, it dances with glee,
Who knew that a nightingale could be so free?

The crickets are laughing, they join in the fun,
A fiesta of chirps, till the day is done.
Swinging from palm trees, they all join the song,
In the heart of the night, nothing can go wrong!

Bats in a flurry, trying to keep pace,
Loop-de-loop flying with a comical grace.
A wiggle, a wobble, they tumble and spin,
They land in the bushes, we laugh at their din!

So here's to the night, with its muses and mirth,
A shindig of creatures, they all share the earth.
With whispers of joy in the soft, starry skies,
We dance to the rhythm, where laughter never dies.

Starlight Over Coral Reefs

The corals are giggling, with colors so bright,
As fish wearing tuxedos glide under the light.
A clownfish is waving, with quite the grand flair,
While a crab with a top hat does jiggles in air.

Turtles take selfies, posing with pride,
While seahorses trot, side by side, side by side.
And here comes a jelly, all wobbly and nice,
Saying, "Join in my dance, it's a slippery slice!"

The octopus sits, looking smart and so wise,
As starfish take turns wearing goofy disguise.
With bubbles a-popping, the laughter runs free,
In the underwater rave, what a sight to see!

Swaying in rhythm, they bounce to the tune,
A bash that would make even mermaids swoon.
With a splash and a giggle, the night carries on,
Under starlit horizons, till the break of dawn.

Silvery Shadows on Sandy Shores

The sands have a secret, they giggle and play,
As waves chase the stars, in a whimsical way.
A crab with a shovel builds castles with flair,
While clams hold a council, debating the air.

A pelican swoops, with a wink and a grin,
Snatching up snacks, with style to begin.
Seagulls are laughing, they steal all the fries,
The beach is alive with mischievous guys!

With flip-flops a-flapping, we run to the sea,
Where all of our worries just vanish—we're free!
The moon is a spotlight, shining down on our crew,
In the world of the kooky, we're crazy but true!

So here's to the shores and the blushing sand,
Where shadows are silly and laughter is grand.
We'll dance with the tide, till the end of the night,
Our hearts filled with joy, in the silver moonlight.

Twilight's Embrace in Paradise

The sun bids adieu, with a wink and a sway,
While the parrots squawk loud, coaxing colors to play.
A monkey in shades, lounging high in a tree,
Sips coconut juice—"Come join the jubilee!"

Even the flowers wear smiles so bright,
As fireflies twinkle, they join in the flight.
With shadows like giggles, they dance on the ground,
While waves hum a tune that is cheerful and round.

The frogs stage a concert, with leaps and with croaks,
As lizards headbang, they're quite the wild blokes.
With a samba and salsa, the night rolls in fun,
In paradise moments, we savor each one!

So lift up your spirits, let joy be the guide,
In twilight's embrace, there's nothing to hide.
With laughter the music, let worries take flight,
In this magical realm, we bask in delight.

Ocean Breeze and Starry Dreams

The waves whisper jokes in the night,
While seagulls dance in full flight.
A crab winks, wearing a top hat,
Joining the conga, imagine that!

Palm trees giggle in the soft glow,
As stars tease us, putting on a show.
The moon rolls by, with a silly face,
And fish start clamoring for some space.

With every splash, a chuckle peeks,
As dolphins plan their stand-up streaks.
In the ocean's lilt, where joy abounds,
Let's laugh along with the silly sounds!

So raise a glass to the night so bright,
Where every shadow has a delight.
Jokes are many, the ocean's our stage,
In this crazy, starry, moonlit page!

Secrets of the Coconut Grove

Coconuts gossip from high above,
Sharing secrets with a push and shove.
One fell down, and what a sight,
He cracked up, laughing at his flight!

Underneath the canopy's shade,
Parrots tell tales about the trade.
"Don't trust the sloths!" they squawk and caw,
"Slow to the punch, they'll leave you in awe!"

The breeze carries whispers of fun,
As monkeys play tag, always on the run.
"Tag, you're it!" they hoot with glee,
While a tortoise roams, longing to flee.

In this grove where giggles collide,
Nature's playground provides the ride.
Come join the laughter, make a stand,
The secrets here are fantastically grand!

Illuminated Horizons at Midnight

Beneath the glow of a lazy sun,
The horizon smiles, it's having fun.
A shrimp writer pens a silly tale,
While a hippo serenades with a sail.

The clouds join in with a fluffy cheer,
"Let's play hide and seek, come here, come near!"
The stars giggle as they count to ten,
Hiding behind the moon once again.

With every wave, a new jingle springs,
As the night sky flutters with bright, silly things.
A band of crabs rocks out on the shore,
Playing conch shells — who could ask for more?

Join the revelry at this hour so late,
Where laughter is plenty and never, just fate.
Dance with the shadows, sway with the breeze,
In this midnight magic, let's all feel at ease!

Starlit Serenades of the Tropics

Beneath the stars, a turtle croons,
Singing ballads of wacky tycoons.
The fish form a band, jamming away,
While mermaids giggle, longing to play.

The fireflies twinkle with rhythmic beats,
Joining in sync on their tiny feet.
"Dancing is easy, just follow along!"
They buzz to the rhythm of a silly song.

A parrot shouts jokes, loud and clear,
While the crabs do the cha-cha, without fear.
The night is alive, with antics galore,
As laughter echoes from the ocean's core.

So let's toast to this magical scene,
Where whimsy reigns, and nothing's routine.
In the heart of the night, let's laugh and sing,
As starlit serenades make our spirits swing!

Echoes of the Night Breeze

The palms sway and giggle, what a sight,
As crabs tap dance under stars so bright.
With coconuts laughing in the tree,
They toss down jokes, quite comically.

The fireflies buzz with a sassy tune,
While frogs croak rhymes, oh what a boon!
The shadows play tag, all in delight,
In a raucous party fueled by the night.

A parrot squawks, wearing shades of green,
Reciting limericks, what a routine!
While the ocean waves join in the jest,
Together they all make the night their fest.

As laughter rises with each salty breeze,
Even the moon can't help but tease.
A chorus of chuckles fills the air,
In this wild, hilarious, moonlit affair.

When Waves Embrace the Darkness

The waves play tricks, they whisper and yawn,
Mischief abounds with each midnight dawn.
They tickle the beach with a splash and a roll,
As sea turtles giggle and lose control.

Each swell brings secrets, with a wink and a sway,
Crabs tell stories of their wild day.
The stars are the witness to this ocean jest,
Where every splash is a hearty fest.

The dolphins leap, with a grin so wide,
Leading the choir through the sea's dark tide.
With a twist and a turn, they dance in sync,
Sipping moonlight smoothies, don't you think?

As shadows dance under the watchful glow,
The ocean's laughter echoes, putting on a show.
In waves of joy, the night holds no fright,
Just fun and frolic in the dark of the night.

Lanterns of the Sea

Lanterns bobble on the restless waves,
Fish in tuxedos dance like brave knaves.
The shrimp wear hats, all stylish and neat,
As they twirl and swirl on their tiny feet.

There's a party down deep where bubbles rise,
With starfish jesters in shimmering ties.
The octopus leads the conga line,
While jellyfish float like toys that shine.

With glowing smiles, they share a treat,
Seaweed snacks and crustacean sweets.
The conch shells giggle, what a delight,
In this underwater waltz, oh so light.

As lantern light flickers on the sea floor,
The laughter of fish fills the ocean's roar.
In this watery realm, joy knows no bounds,
As the merry sea creatures do happy rounds.

Twilight Florals and Distant Echoes

The flowers bloom with a cheeky charm,
Grinning at bees, spreading sweet balm.
With petals that wiggle in the gentle breeze,
They plot with the crickets, causing mischief with ease.

A cactus throws shade with a playful poke,
While daisies burst forth with a silly joke.
The nightingale's chirps keep the fun alive,
As the garden dances, fragrant and thrive.

With butterflies twirling in a joyous flight,
They chase each other, oh what a sight!
Each fragrance whispers, a tale of delight,
In this magical place, under starlit night.

As the moon peeks down with a teasing grin,
The flowers chuckle, inviting us in.
For in their kingdom, laughter will soar,
And echo through evenings forevermore.

Luminous Secrets of the Island

Under banana leaves, I chase a bright glare,
A crab takes a selfie, with not a single care.
Coconuts giggle, they swing from a vine,
While parrots throw shade, as they parse out the fine.

The moon spins tales, like a fish on a hook,
In flip-flops, I'm tripping, so please take a look.
The stars throw a party, all glitzy and grand,
As I juggle my drinks, with a slip of my hand.

Laughter erupts from a coconut stand,
A cat plays the drums with a skill that's quite grand.
With each clumsy step, I'm a sight to behold,
The island keeps laughing, our secrets unfold.

As twilight descends, the night gets a glow,
With winks from the crabs that put on quite the show.
I dance with the shadows, in flip-flop design,
In this luminous realm, it's all perfectly fine.

Dreams Adrift on Ocean Waves

Surfboards are smiling, the sea's got a grin,
As jellyfish jiggle, in bubbles we spin.
My floatie's rebellious, it flops and it flails,
Making friends with a fish—oh, the oceanic tales!

Seagulls are teaming, they plot and they plan,
To steal all my popcorn, like a part of their clan.
With a splash and a laugh, the sun takes a dive,
While crabs bring the rhythm, and sharks jive alive.

The breeze whispers secrets of sunburned despair,
As I race on a wave, with seaweed in hair.
The dolphins are chuckling, they leap with delight,
In a dance of pure chaos, beneath stars so bright.

With dreams on the surf, I paddle and sway,
Through giggles of mermaids, who join in the play.
Each wave a reminder, to laugh 'til the end,
In this hilarious drift, where the sea is a friend.

A Serenade Beneath Velvet Skies

Crickets compose tunes, as stars join the show,
A breeze brings the laughter, in ripples it flows.
With moonbeams as notes, we're dancing around,
To the music of night, in this island playground.

The bugs bring the rhythm, in sync, they unite,
As frogs join the chorus, with croaks of delight.
A firefly winks, it's a mischievous sprite,
While I trip on my sandals, oh what a sight!

The palms sway in rhythm, like they know the beat,
While I saunter with grace, embracing my feet.
The ocean's soft whispers, a sweet lullaby,
Catch me napping at dusk, with my dreams sailing high.

With laughter as our anthem, we serenade night,
Under the velvet, where everything's bright.
In this playful parade, the stars seem to wink,
As I splash on the shore, finding more time to think.

Silhouettes Dance in Mango Trees

Underneath mango trees, shadows twist and tease,
With silhouettes grooving, swaying in the breeze.
A dog in a tutu steals all of the show,
While I slip on a mango, oh where did it go?

The stars take their places, a stage full of charms,
As fireflies twinkle, like lights in our arms.
A parrot named Charlie gets frisky tonight,
His dance is so funky, it's out of all sight!

The night blooms with laughter, as fruit bats take flight,
In the chaos of dance, we're all feeling right.
Jumpsuits of shadows, we slide and we glide,
In this mango-lit fiesta, come join for the ride!

With giggles and wiggles, we bounce 'neath the light,
As silhouettes have fun, beneath stars shining bright.
In the tangle of branches, we chime with the sound,
Of laughter and joy, as our happiness bounds.

Moonlit Palms Swaying Softly

Beneath the starry, winking eyes,
The palms are swaying, oh what a surprise!
A monkey swings by, wearing a hat,
He thinks he's the king — imagine that!

A coconut drops with a loud plop,
The party's alive, and it won't stop!
In the warm breeze, a lizard dines,
Counting the stars like dollar signs.

Coconuts rolling on the sandy shore,
They giggle and bounce — oh, hear them roar!
The crabs do the hustle, quite a sight,
Dancing their hearts out beneath the night.

So raise your cup and toast the scene,
To monkeys in caps and a midnight routine!
For in this place of joy and cheer,
A laugh and a jig are always near.

The Dance of Fireflies in Dusk

Under a curtain of violet hues,
Fireflies twirl, it's quite the news!
They twinkle and sparkle, a blinking crew,
Join in their dance — what else can you do?

A frog in the chorus says, 'Ribbit, now!'
While a cat joins the fun, somehow,
With goggles on, she leaps in bliss,
'What a strange world to enter, I must admit!'

The flies make patterns like a wacky show,
A disco ball dance floor all aglow!
As they weave through the air with glee,
You'd think they're holding the best jamboree.

So twirl with the bugs and lose your fear,
For under dusk's glow, the fun is clear!
Each flicker a chuckle, a wink, a tease —
In this warm evening, let's dance with ease!

Nightfall's Kiss on Exotic Blooms

In the garden where the shadows play,
Exotic blooms giggle at the end of the day.
A parrot overhears their floral chat,
He squawks with laughter — oh, imagine that!

The lilies in white wear shoes made of dew,
While orchids in pink paint the night anew.
'Let's have a ball!' the roses call,
As a breeze stirs up a floral brawl.

With petals so soft, they sway in delight,
Tickled by whispers of a playful night.
Bees join the dance, buzzing their tune,
It's a party for flowers beneath the moon!

So here's to the blooms with their giggly spree,
In laughter and color, they feel so free!
With each nightfall's kiss, their spirits ignite,
In this garden of charm, everything feels right.

Mysteries Beneath the Gleaming Night

Beneath the stars, a turtle sneaks,
With shades on, he thinks he's sleek!
On his back, he carries a disco light,
Shining bright as he waddles in the night.

The waves chuckle softly while the crabs sway,
A game of hide and seek in the spray.
The seaweed giggles, tickling toes,
As a fish in a hat grins, 'Here it goes!'

Octopus in a bow tie, what a sight!
Trying his best to dance tonight.
With eight legs busy getting it wrong,
He twirls and tumbles, but loves the song!

So join the parade of quirky delight,
In the gleam of the moon, everything feels right.
With laughs and odd moves, let's take flight,
In this world of wonders, through the night.

www.ingramcontent.com/pod-product-compliance
Lightning Source LLC
Chambersburg PA
CBHW072134070526
44585CB00016B/1673